I0485546

COLOR TEST PAGE

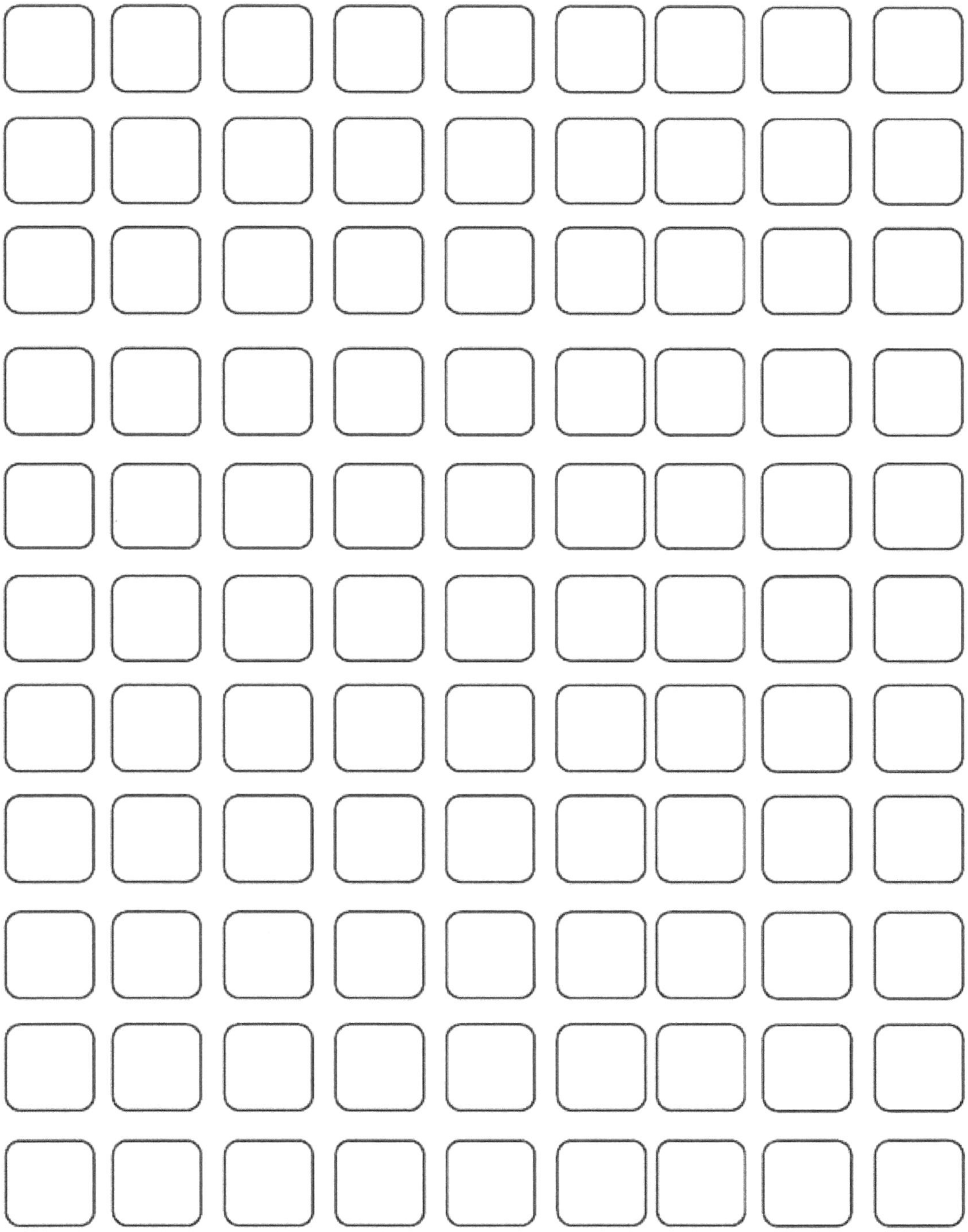

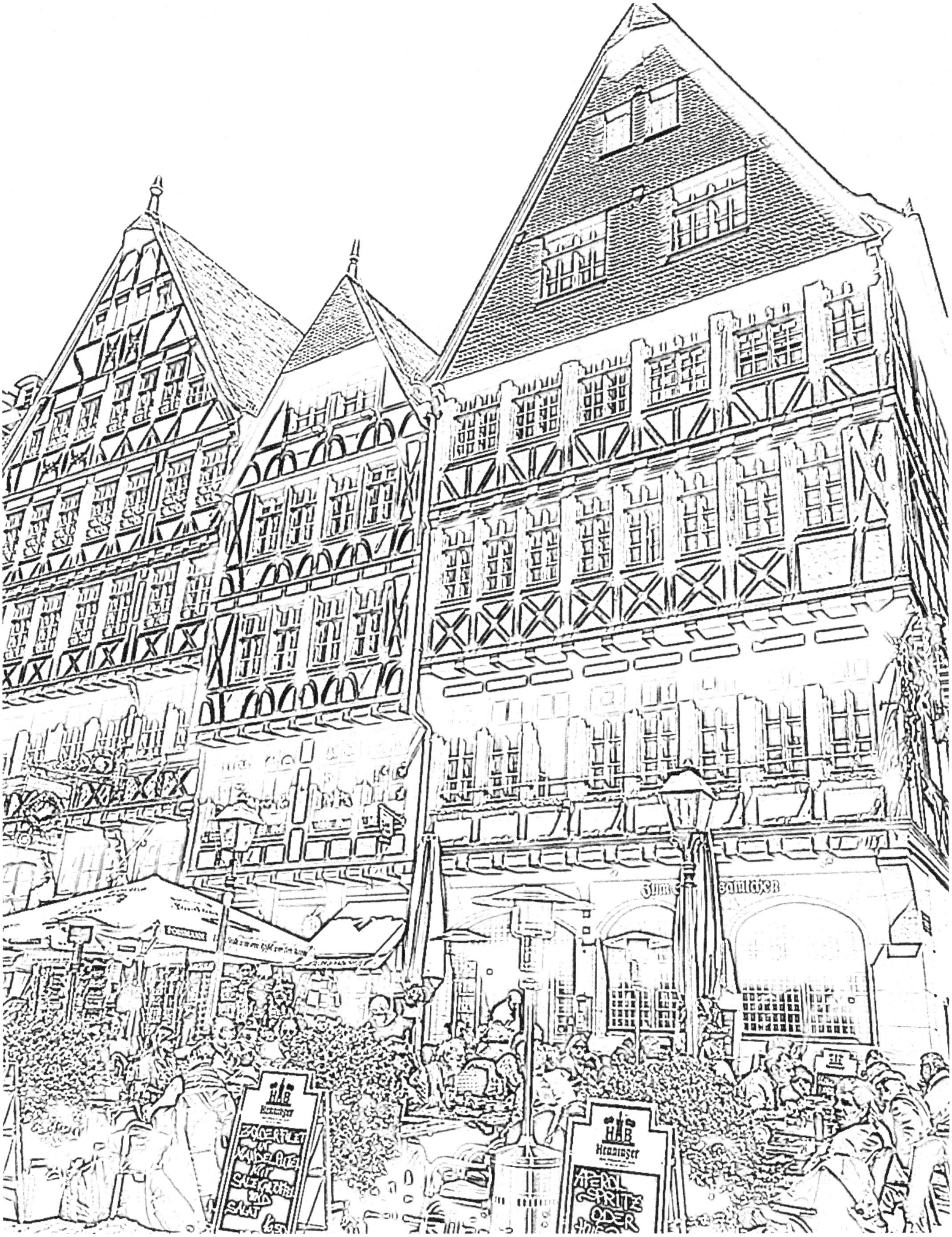

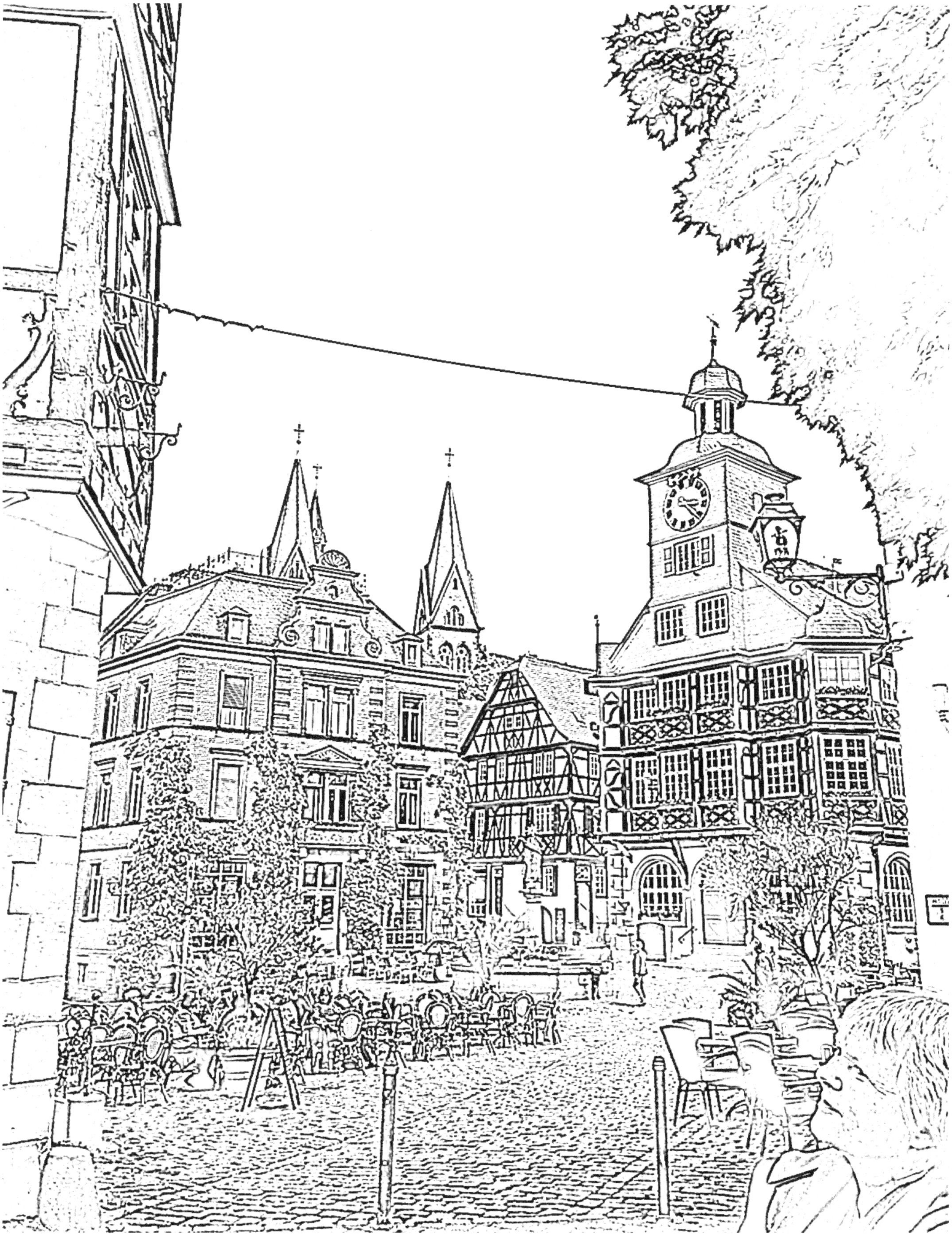

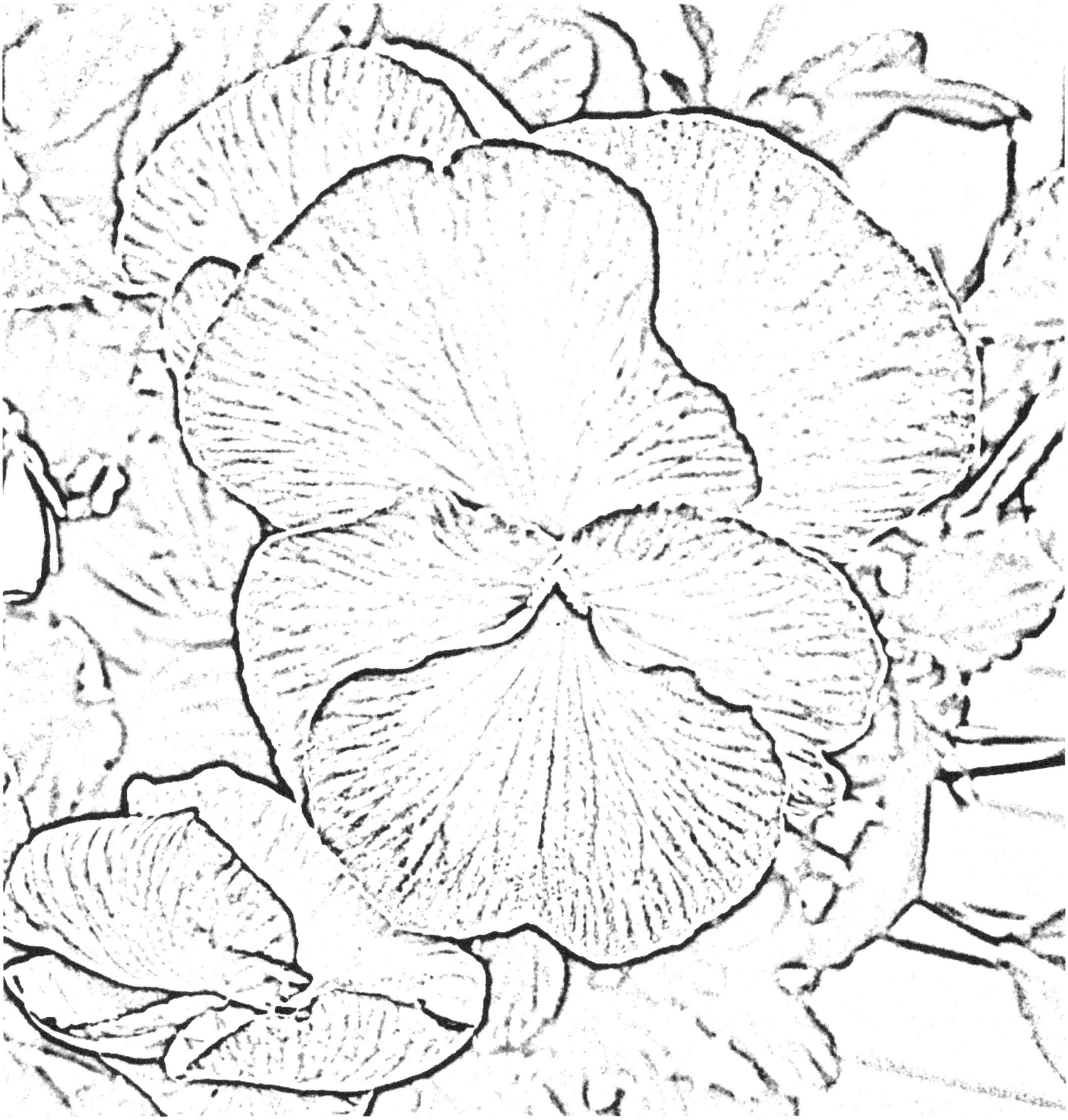

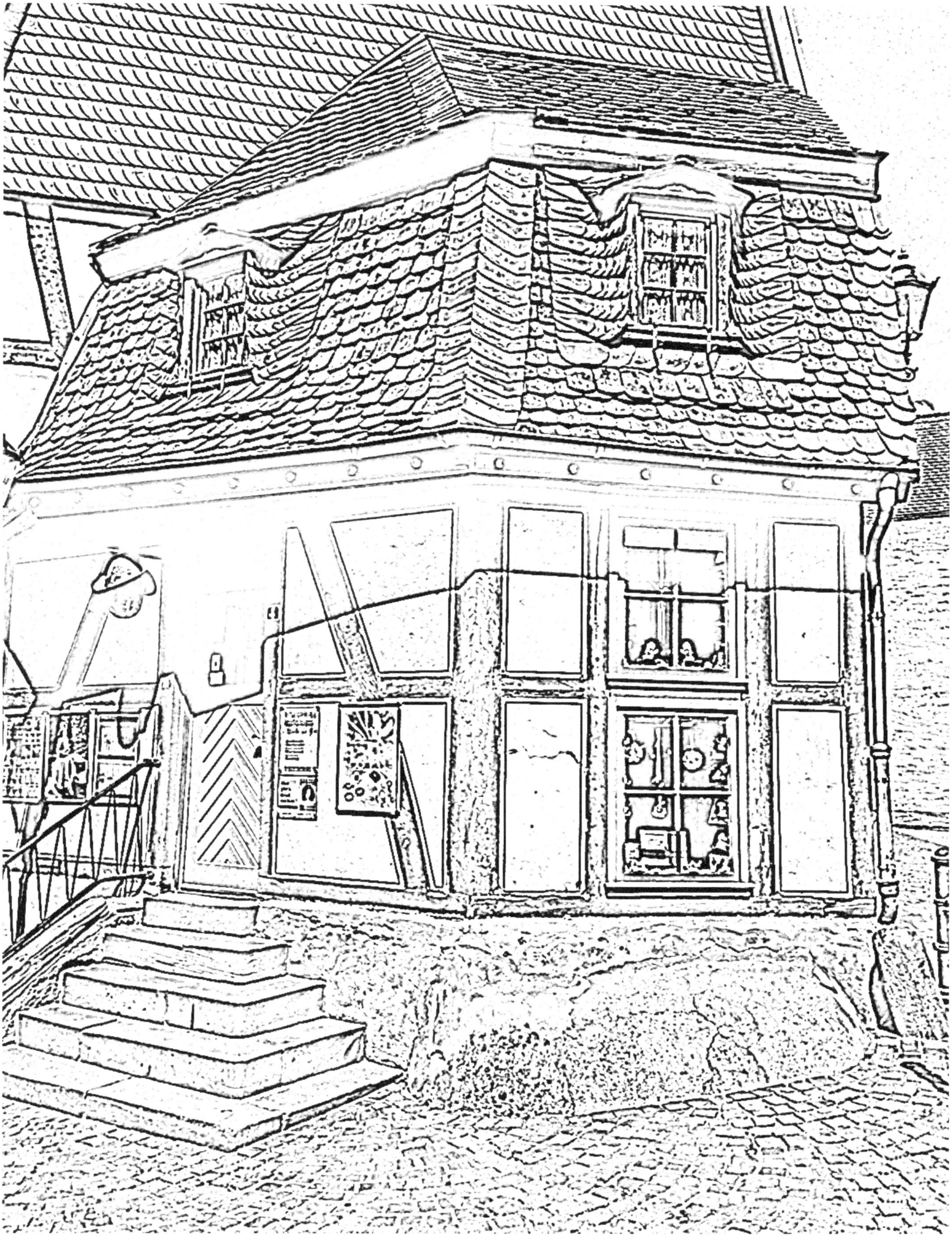

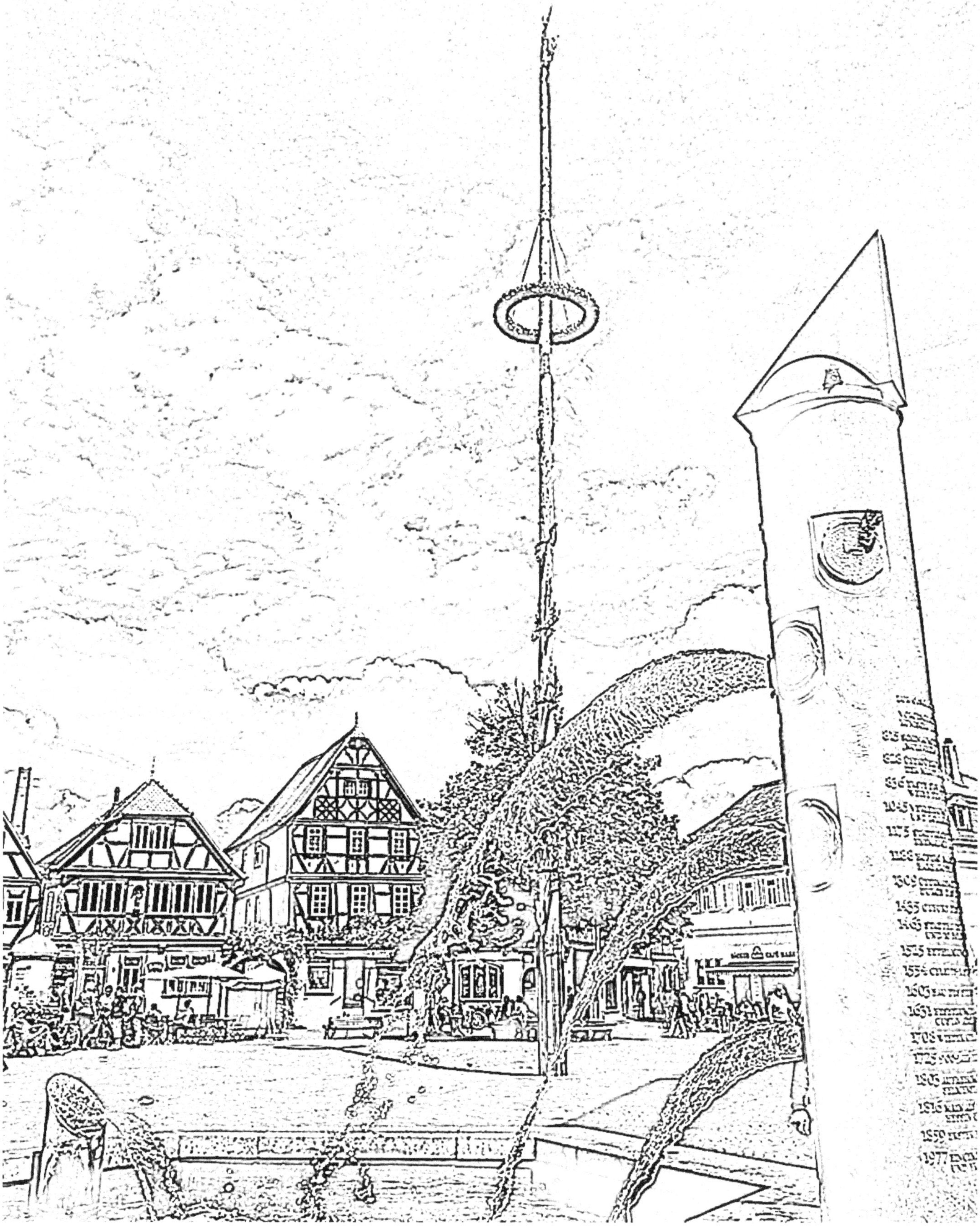

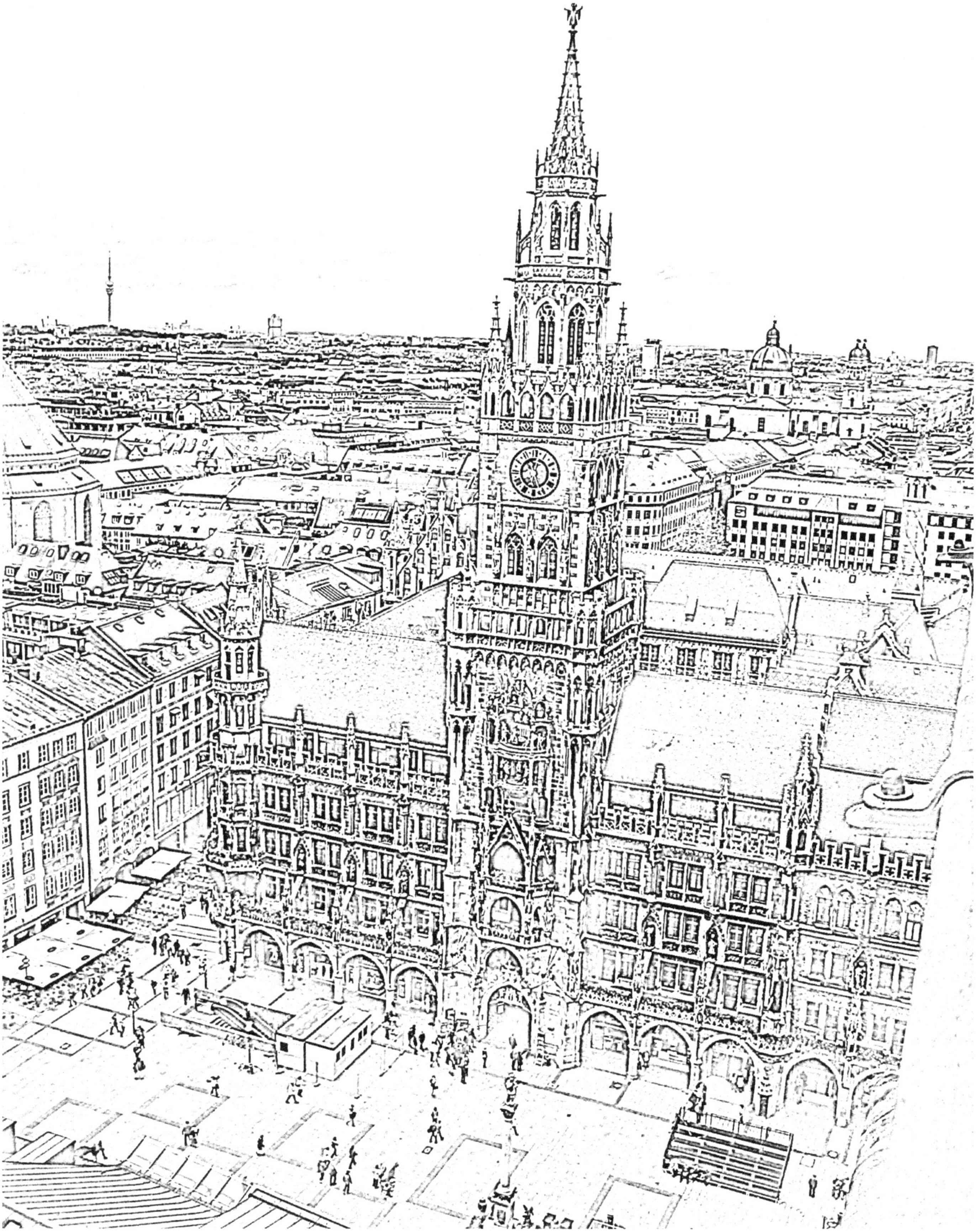

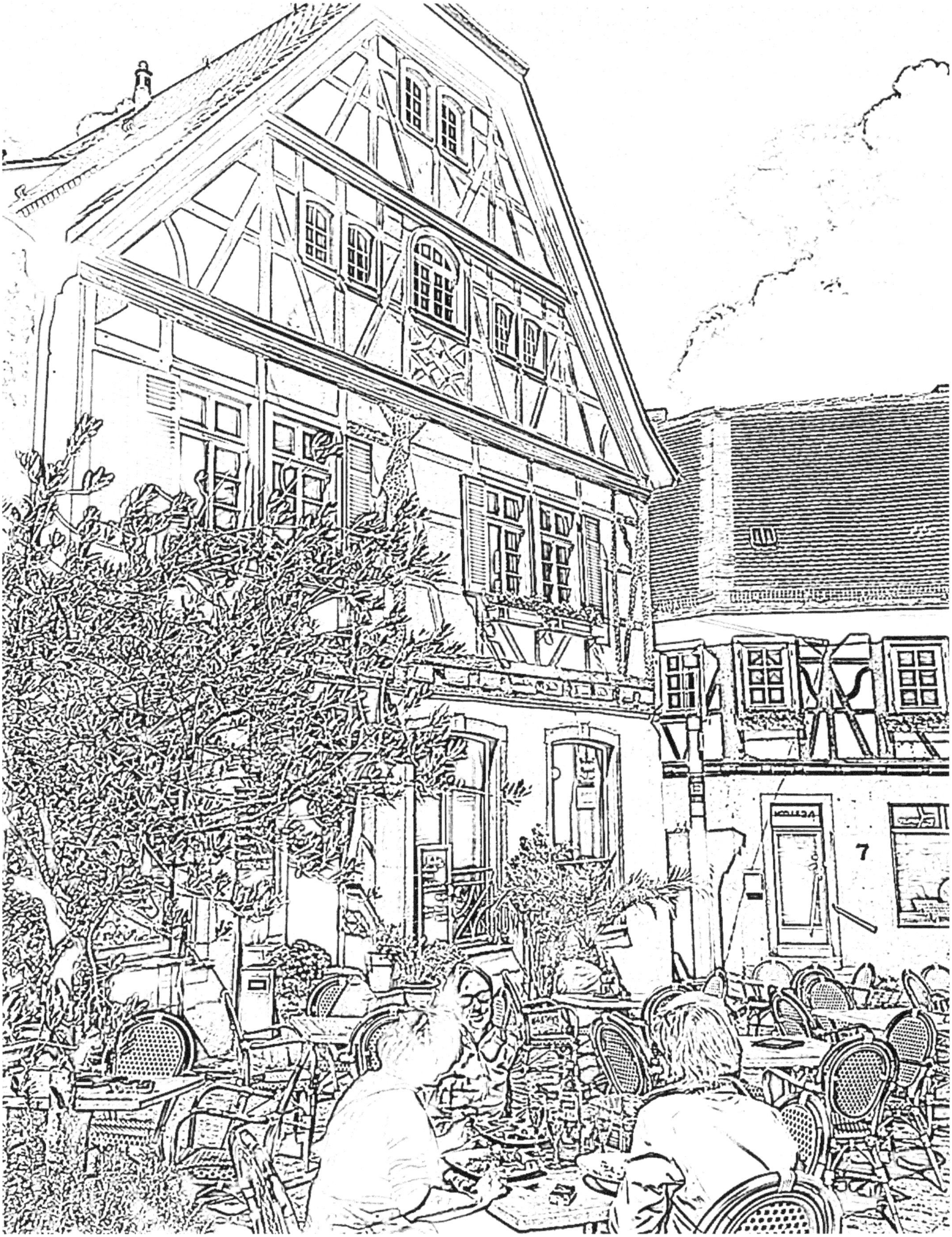
7

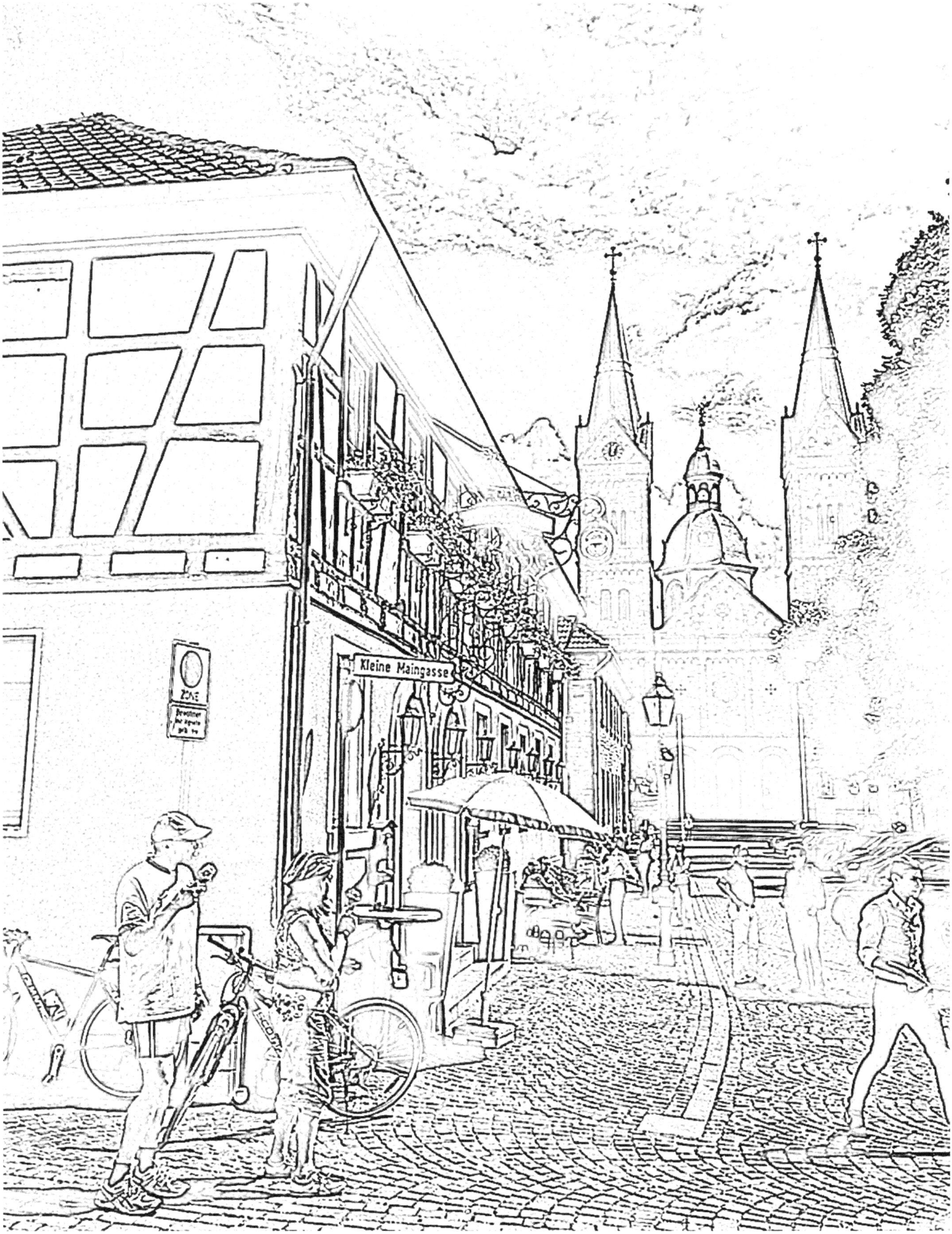
Kleine Maingasse
ZONE

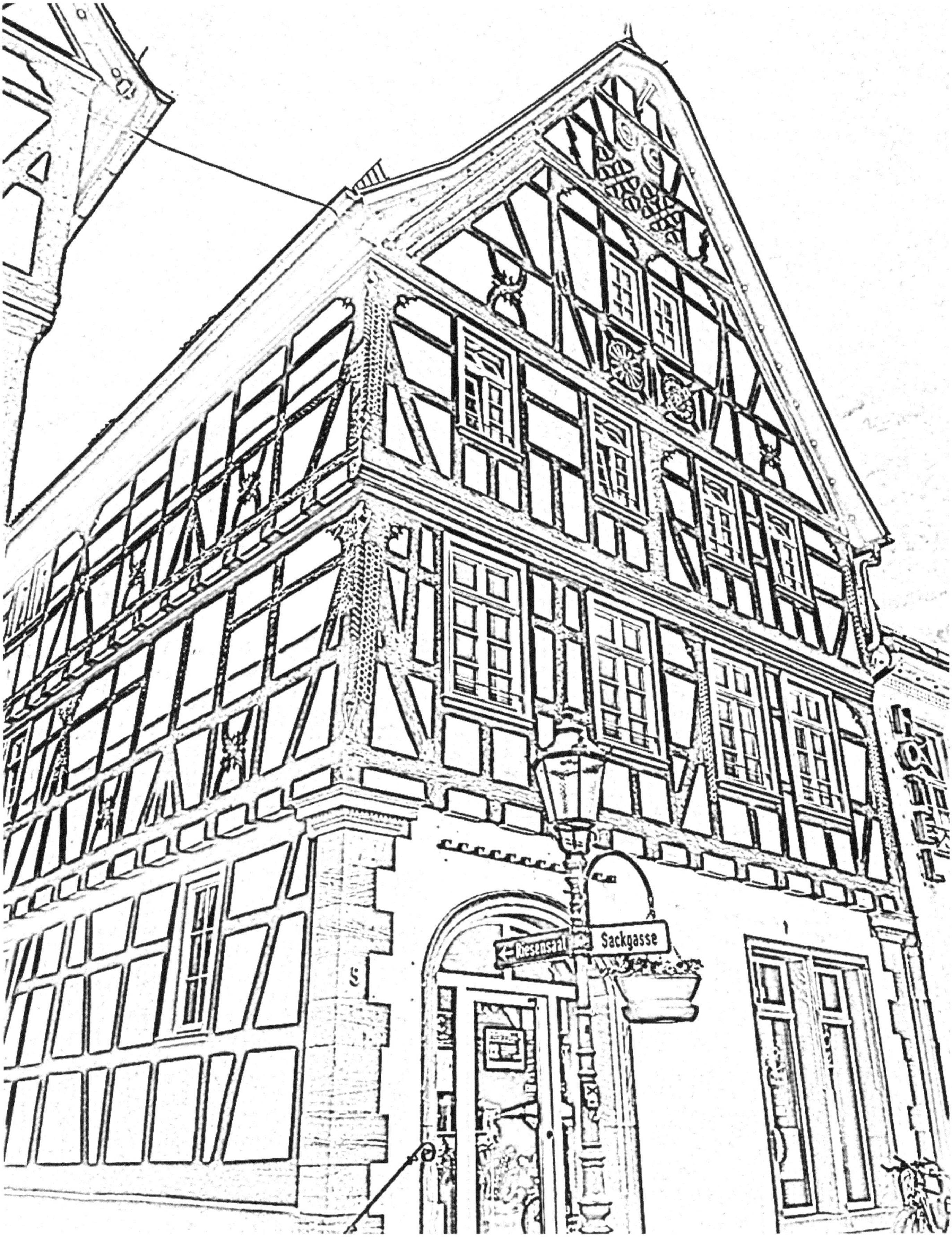
Sackgasse

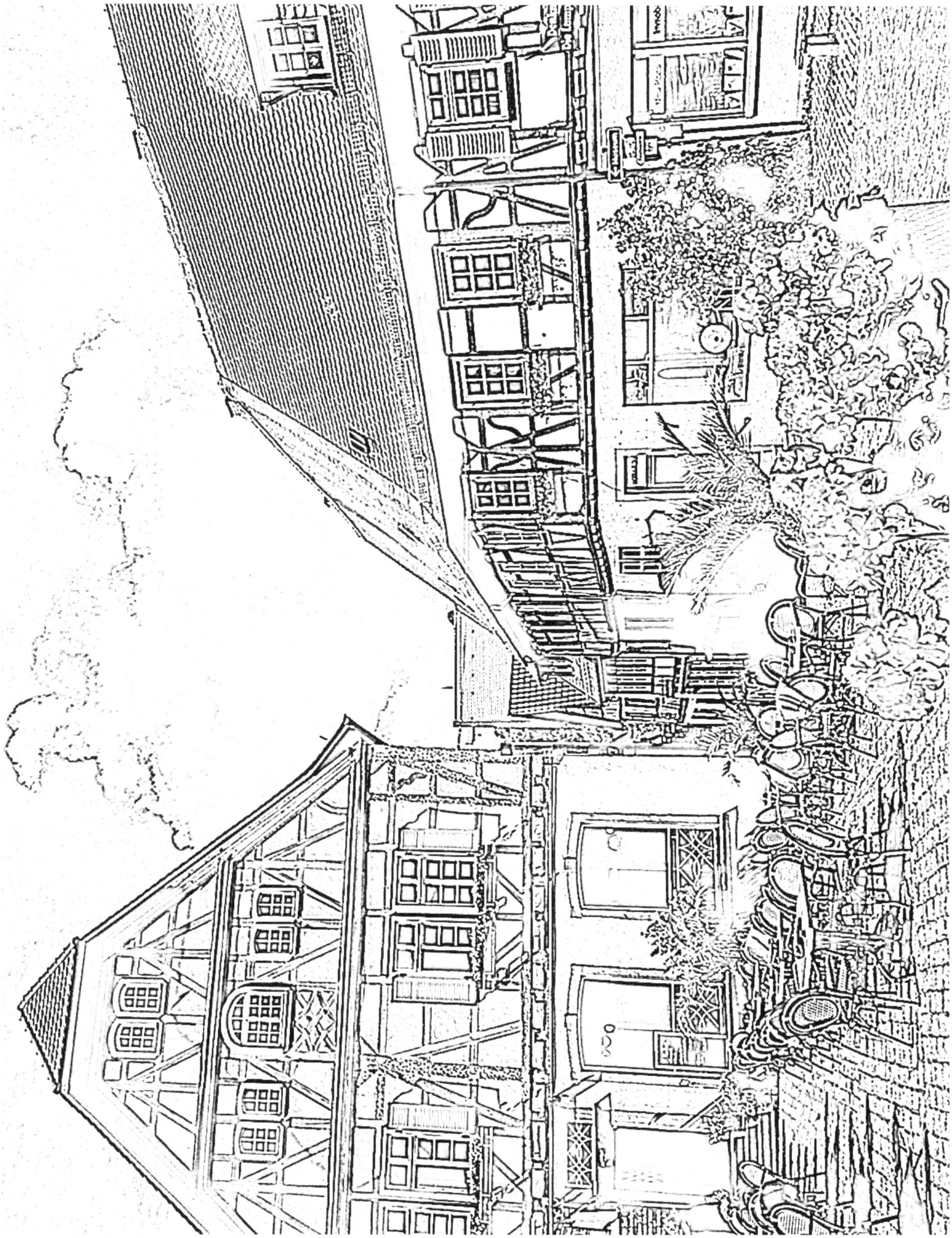

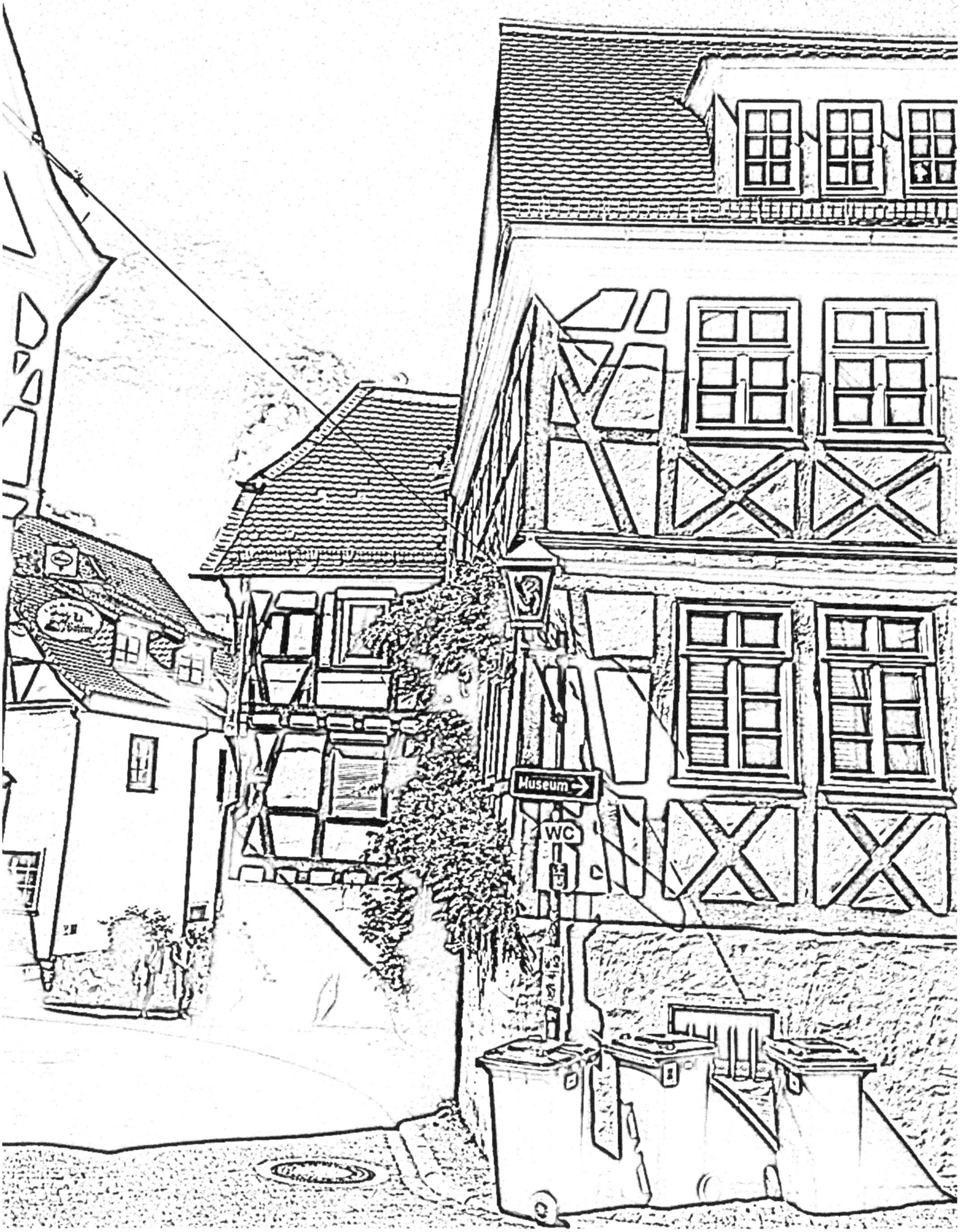
Museum
WC

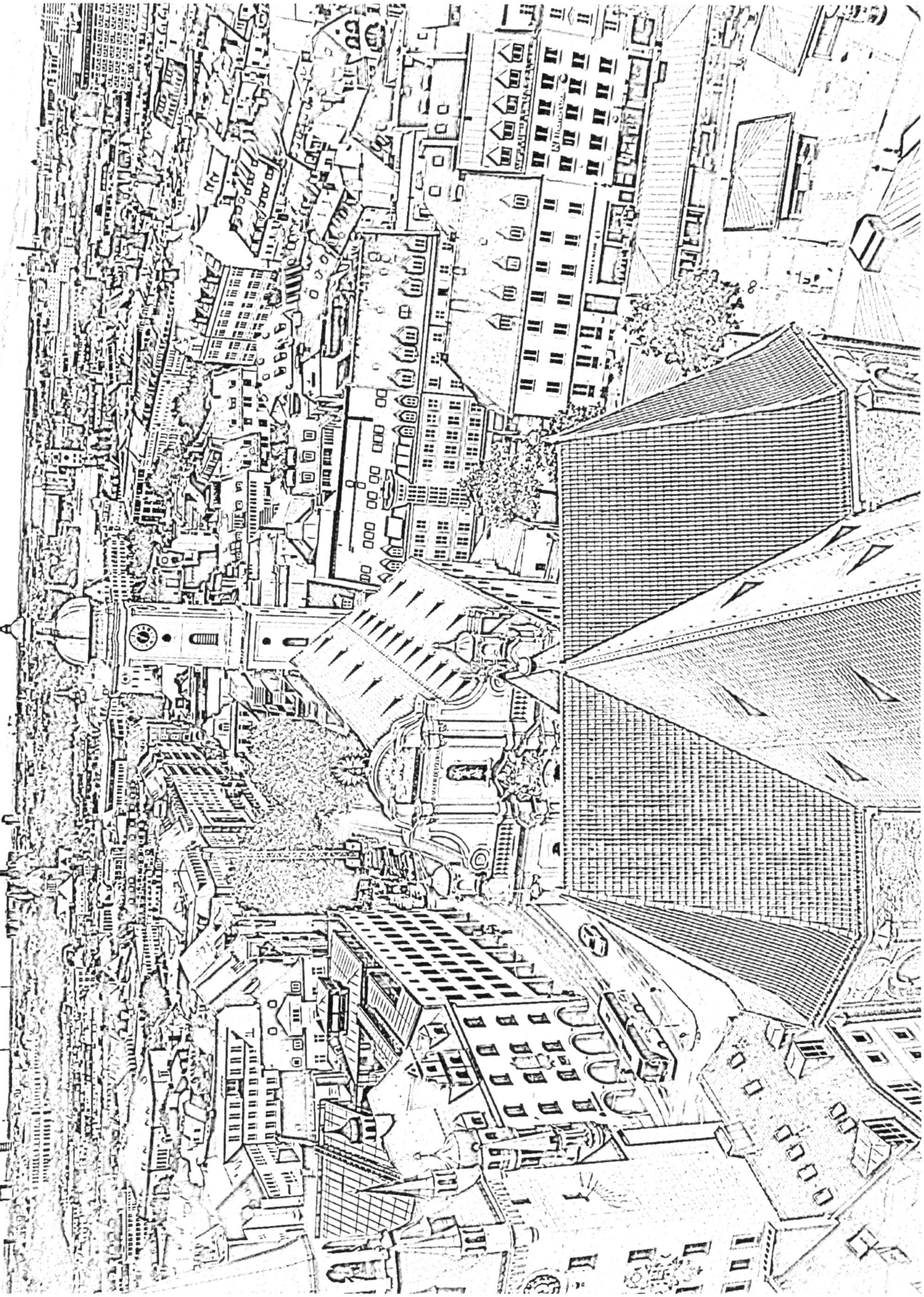

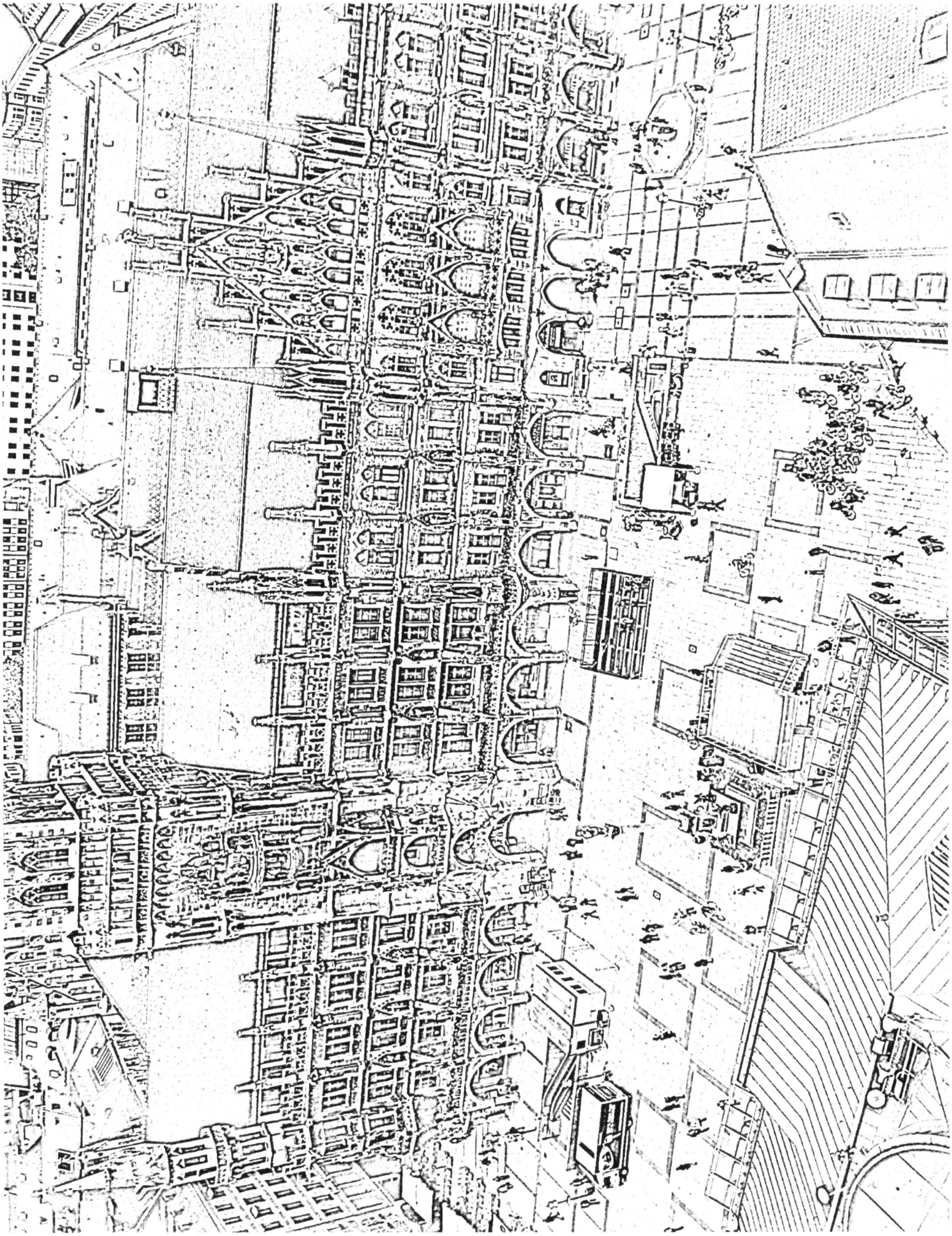

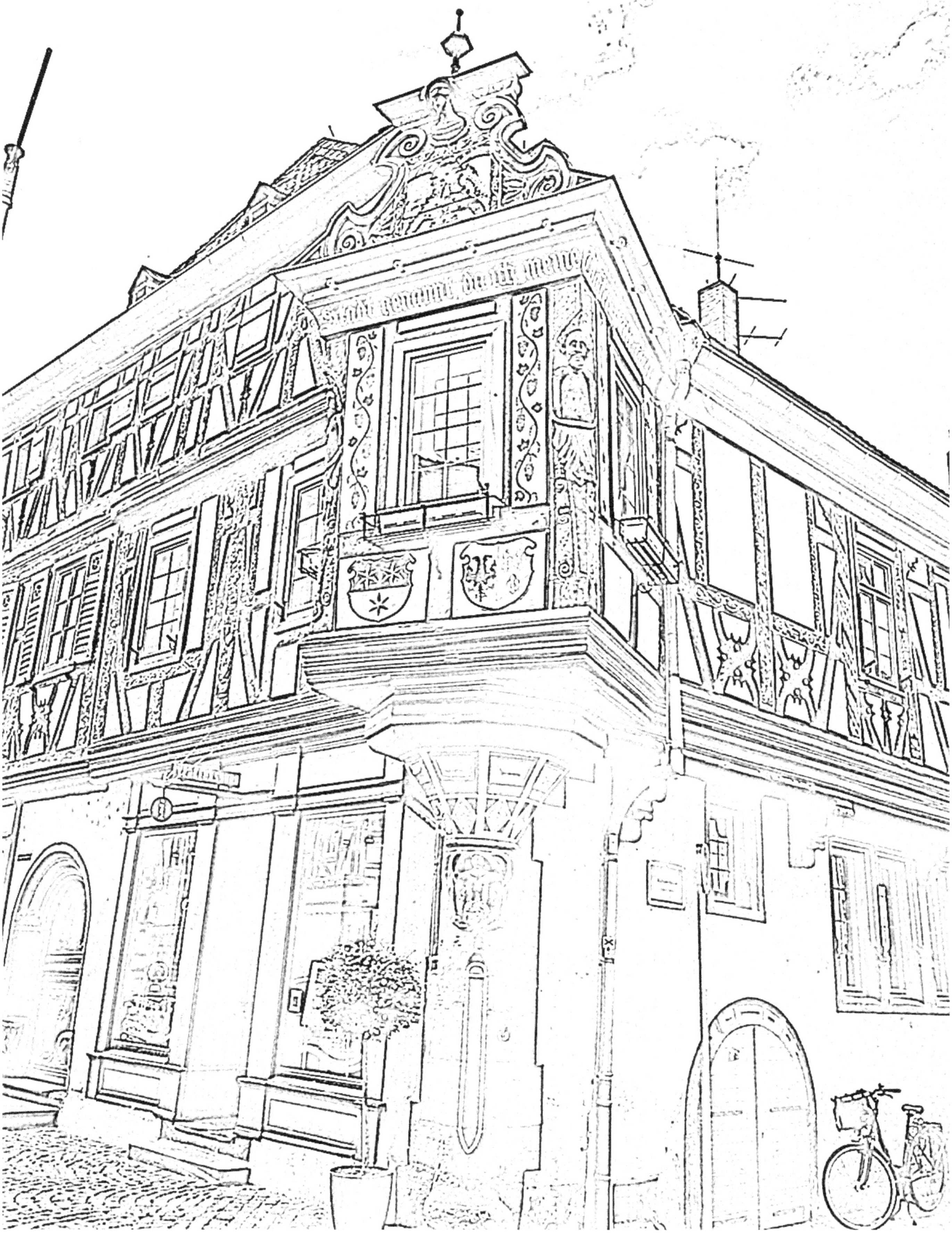

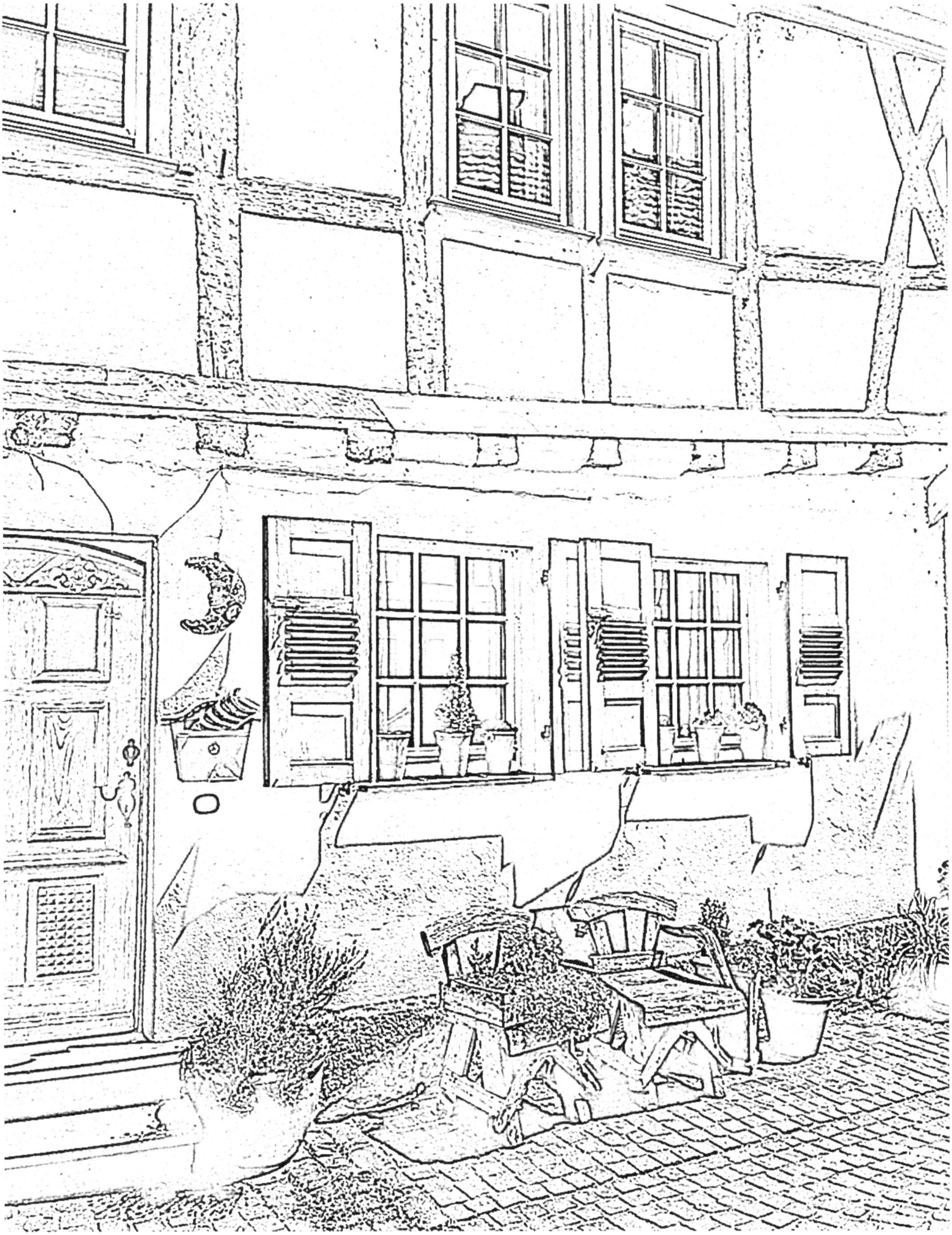

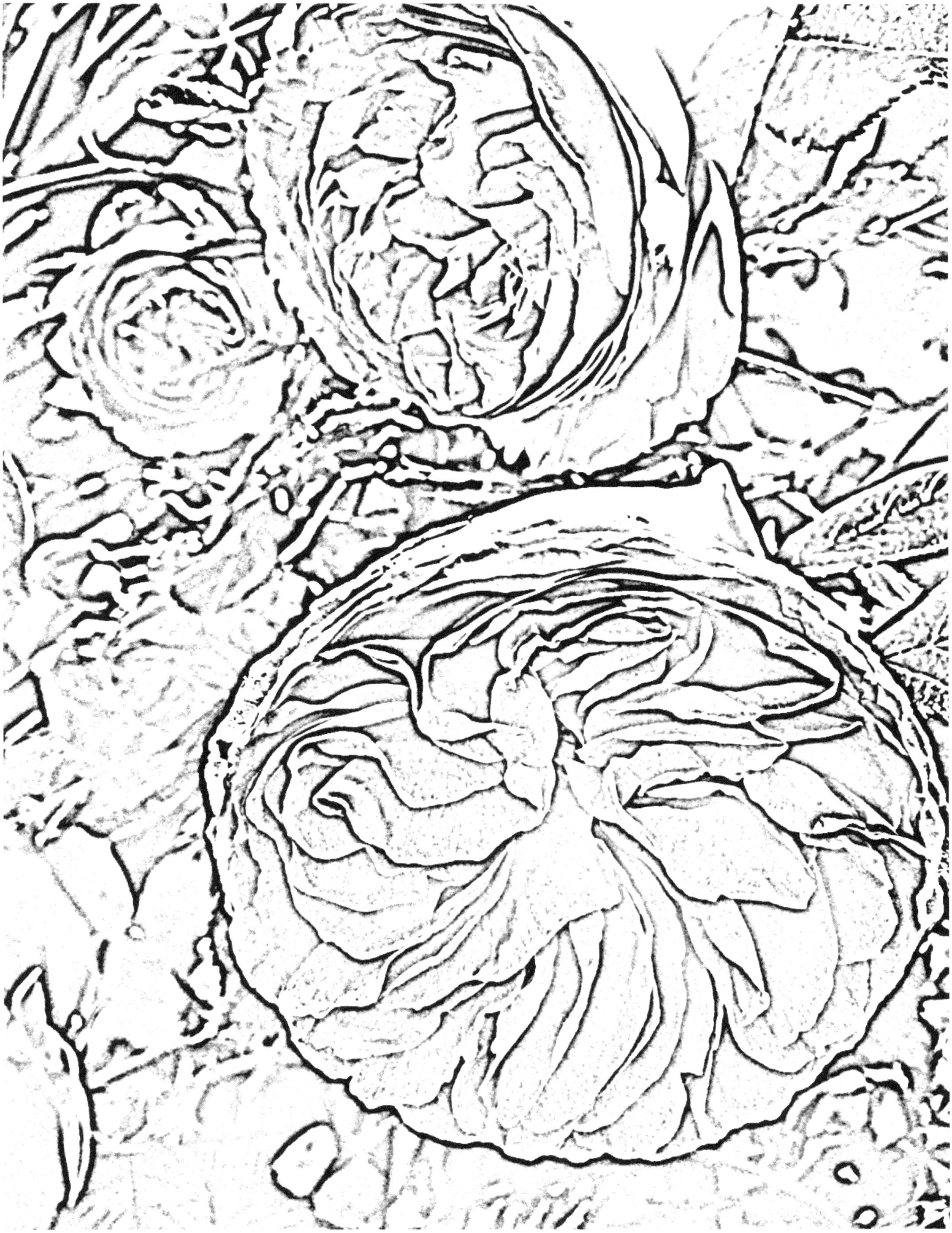

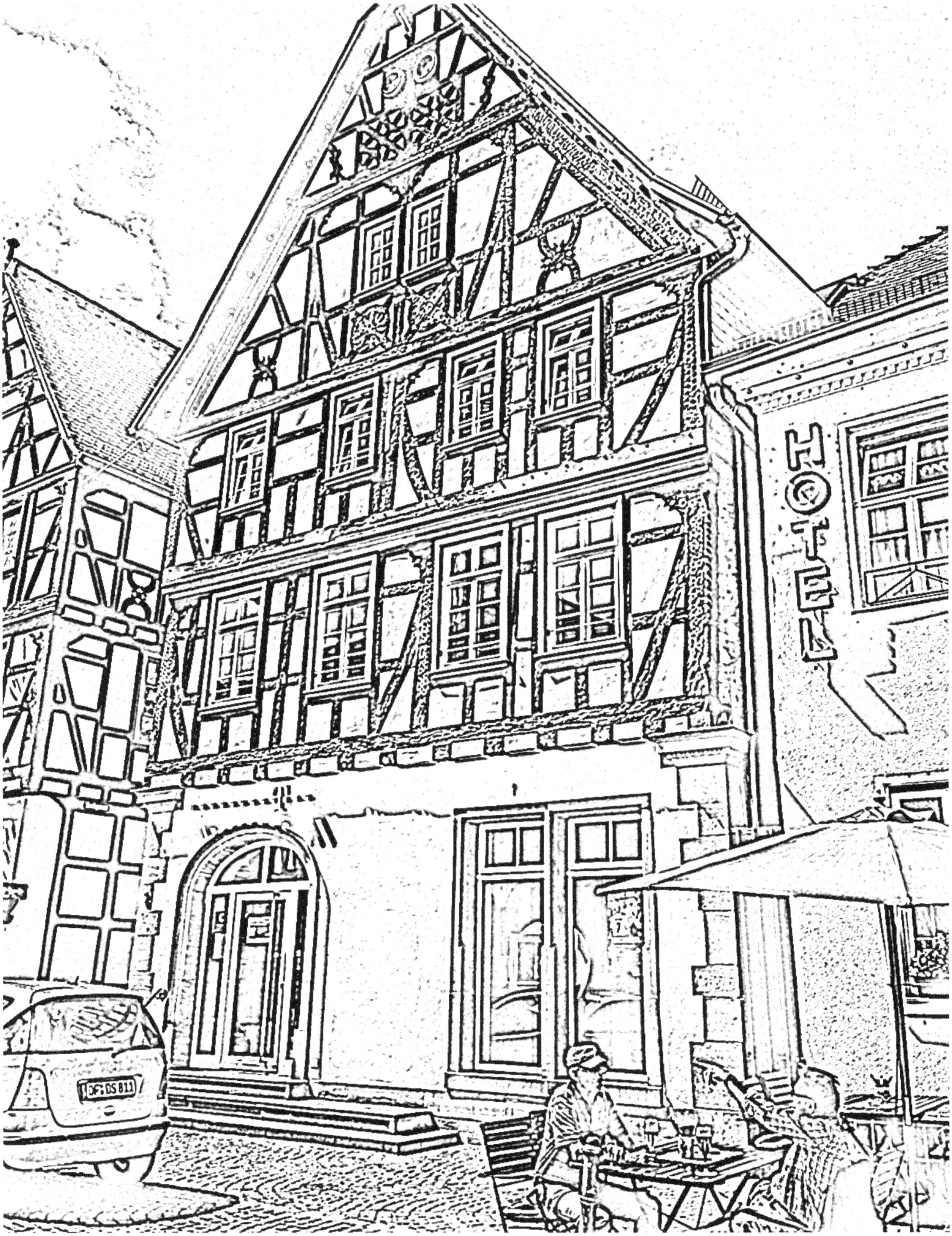
HOTEL

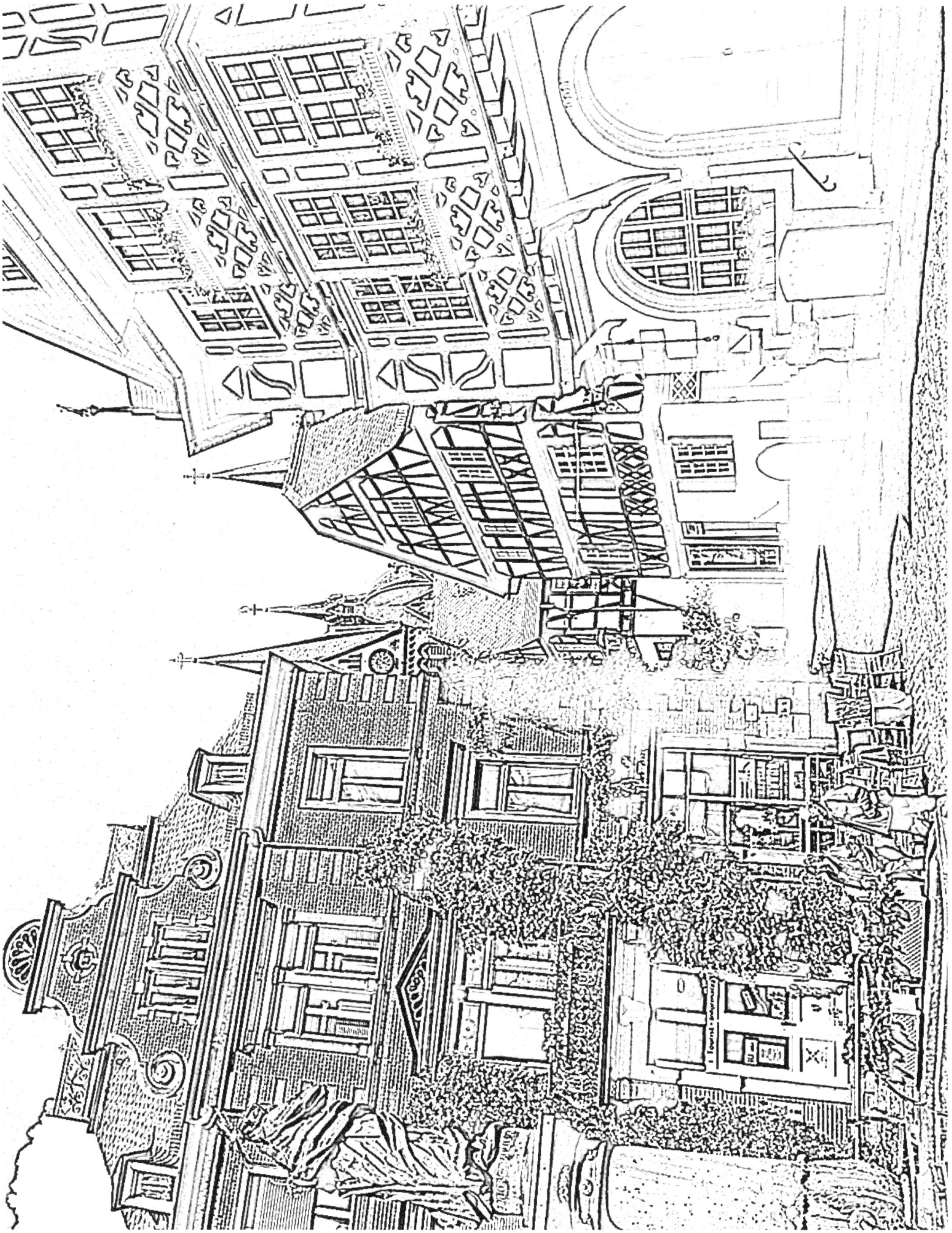

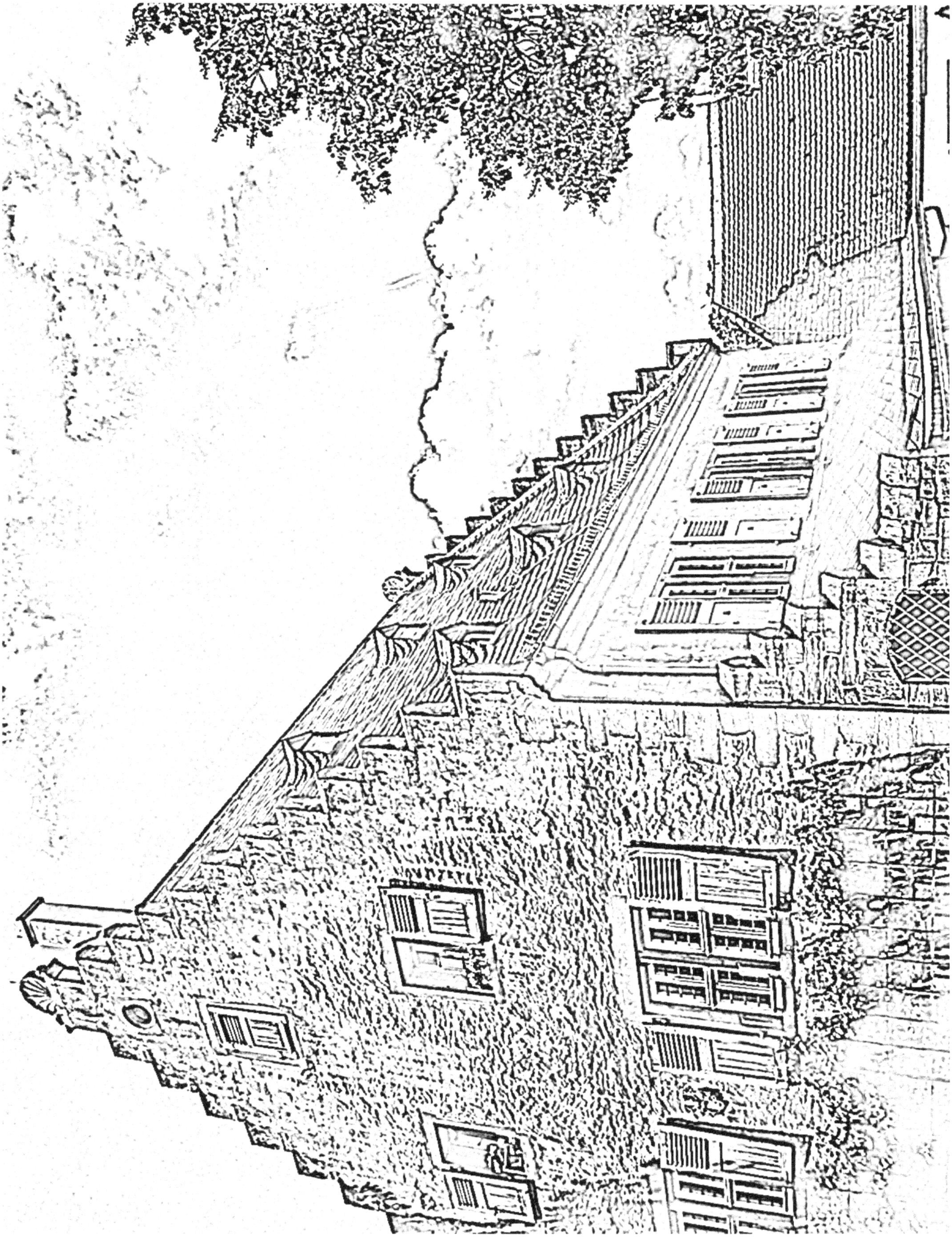

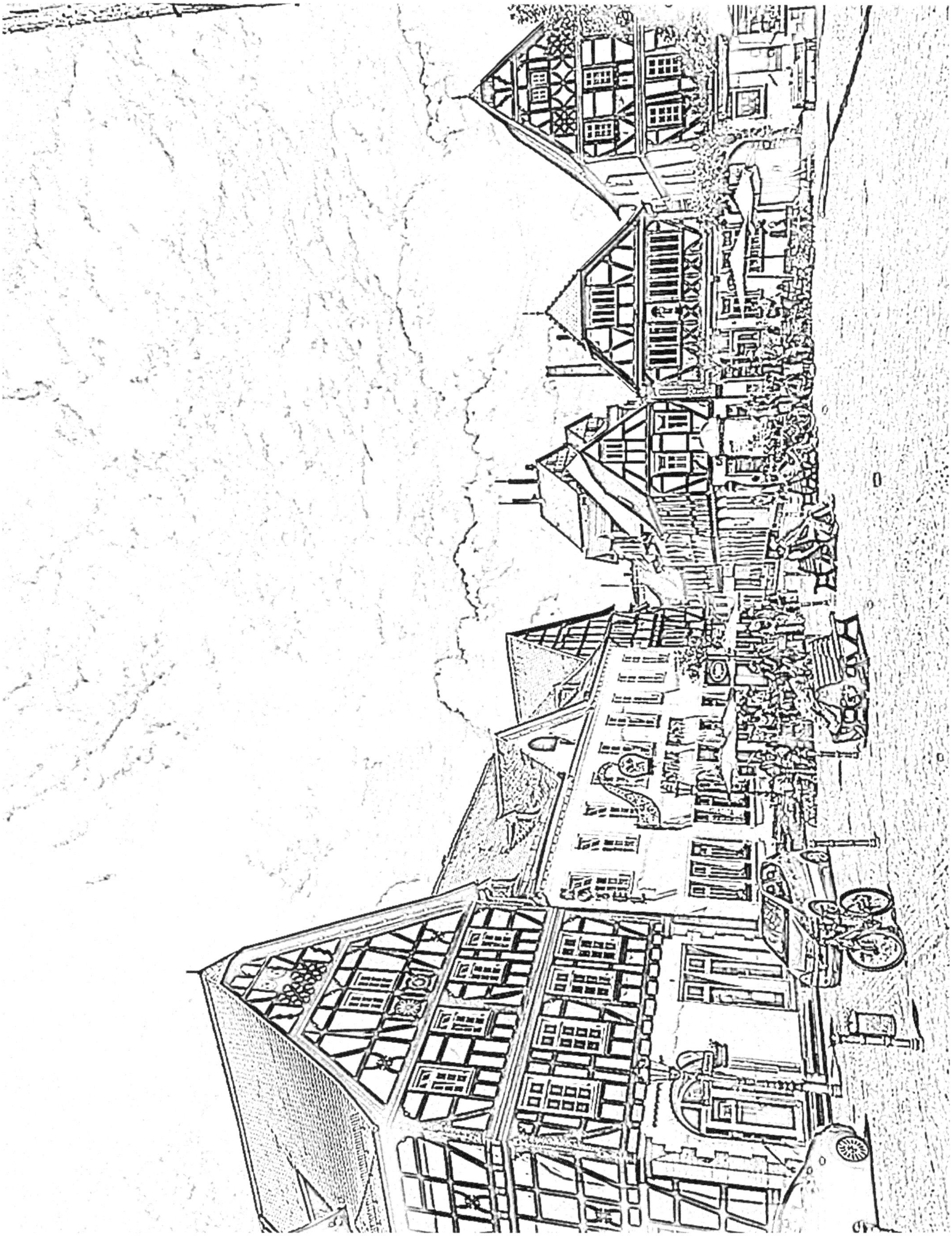

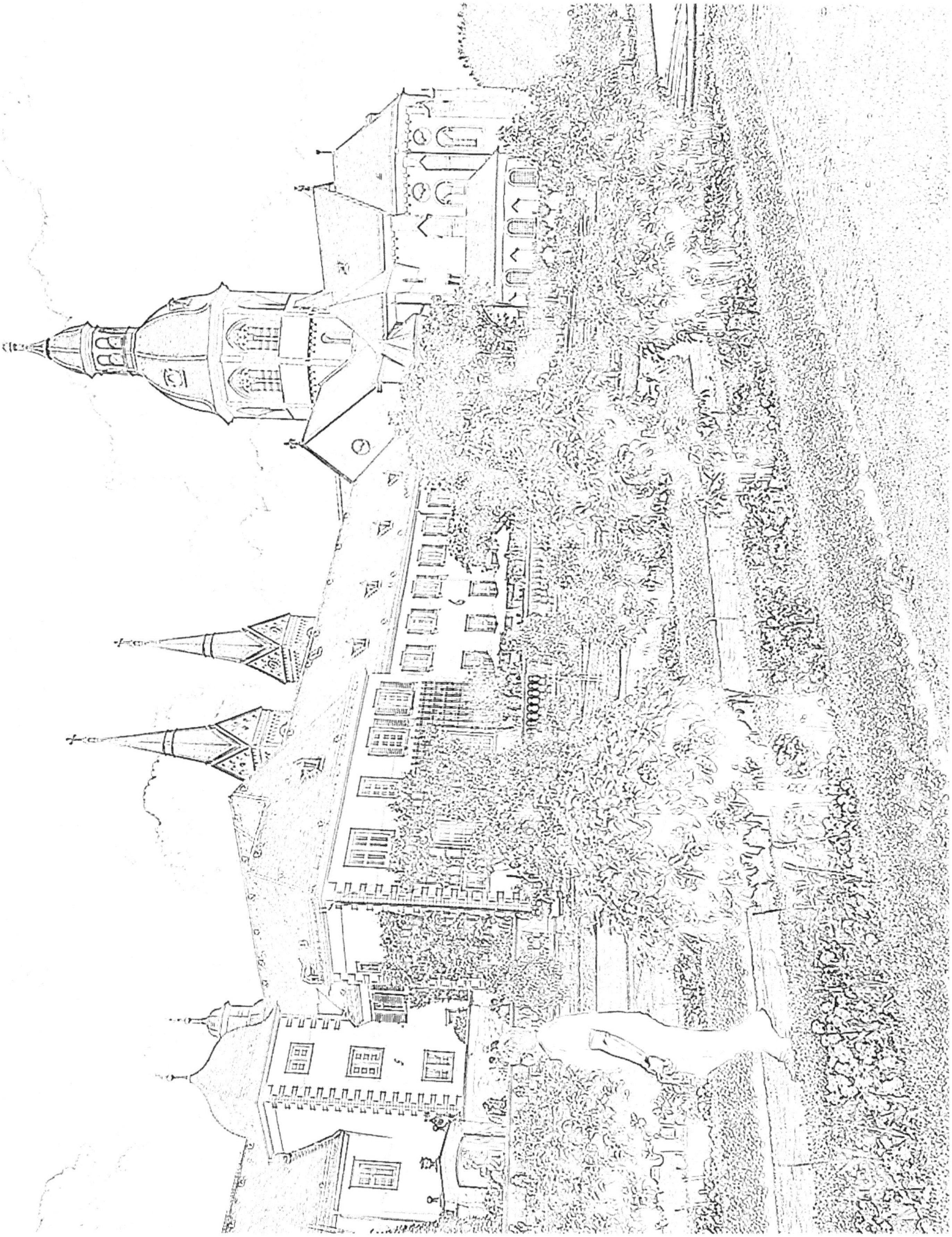

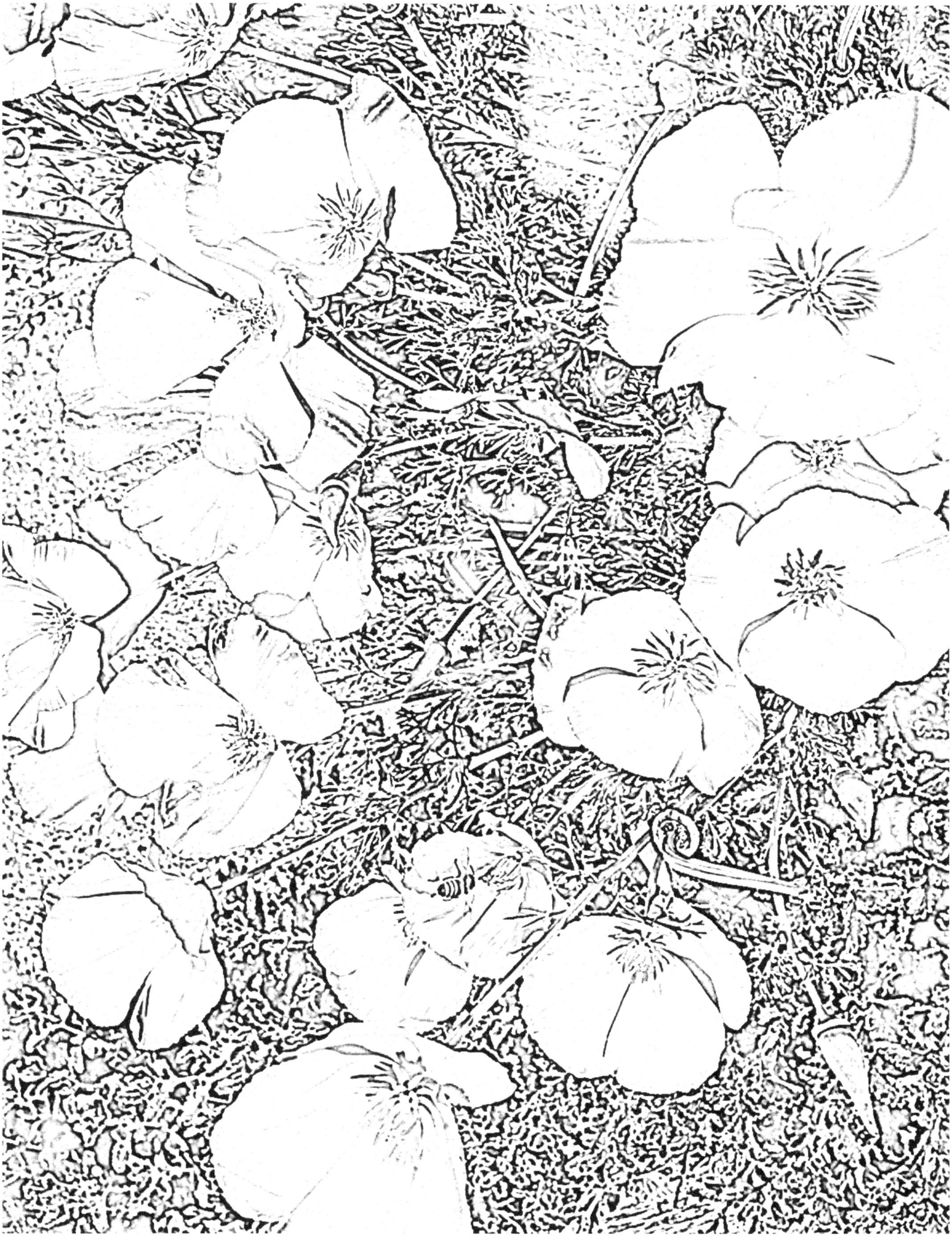

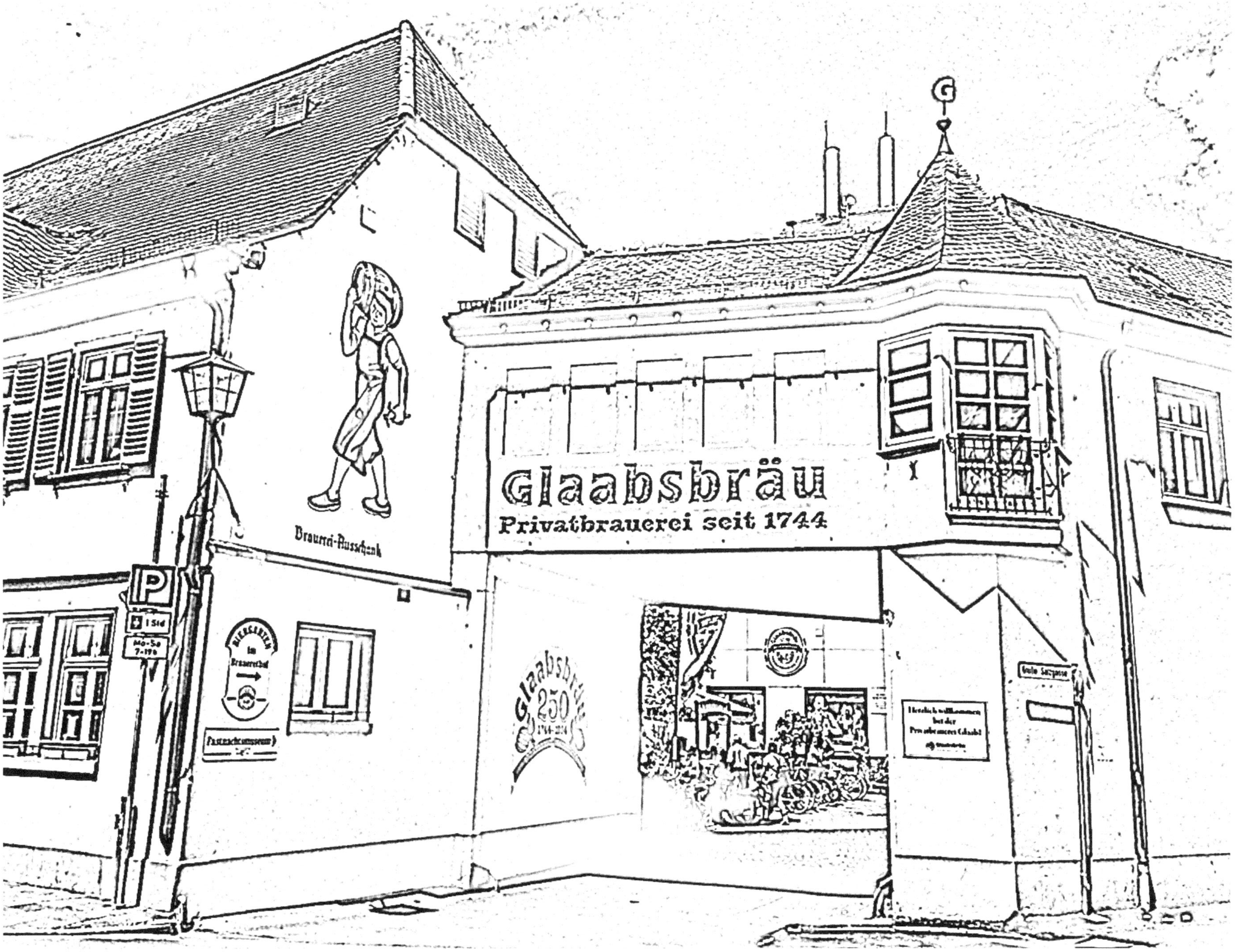
Glaabsbräu
Privatbrauerei seit 1744
Brauerei-Ausschank
P
Glaabsbräu
250
1744-1994

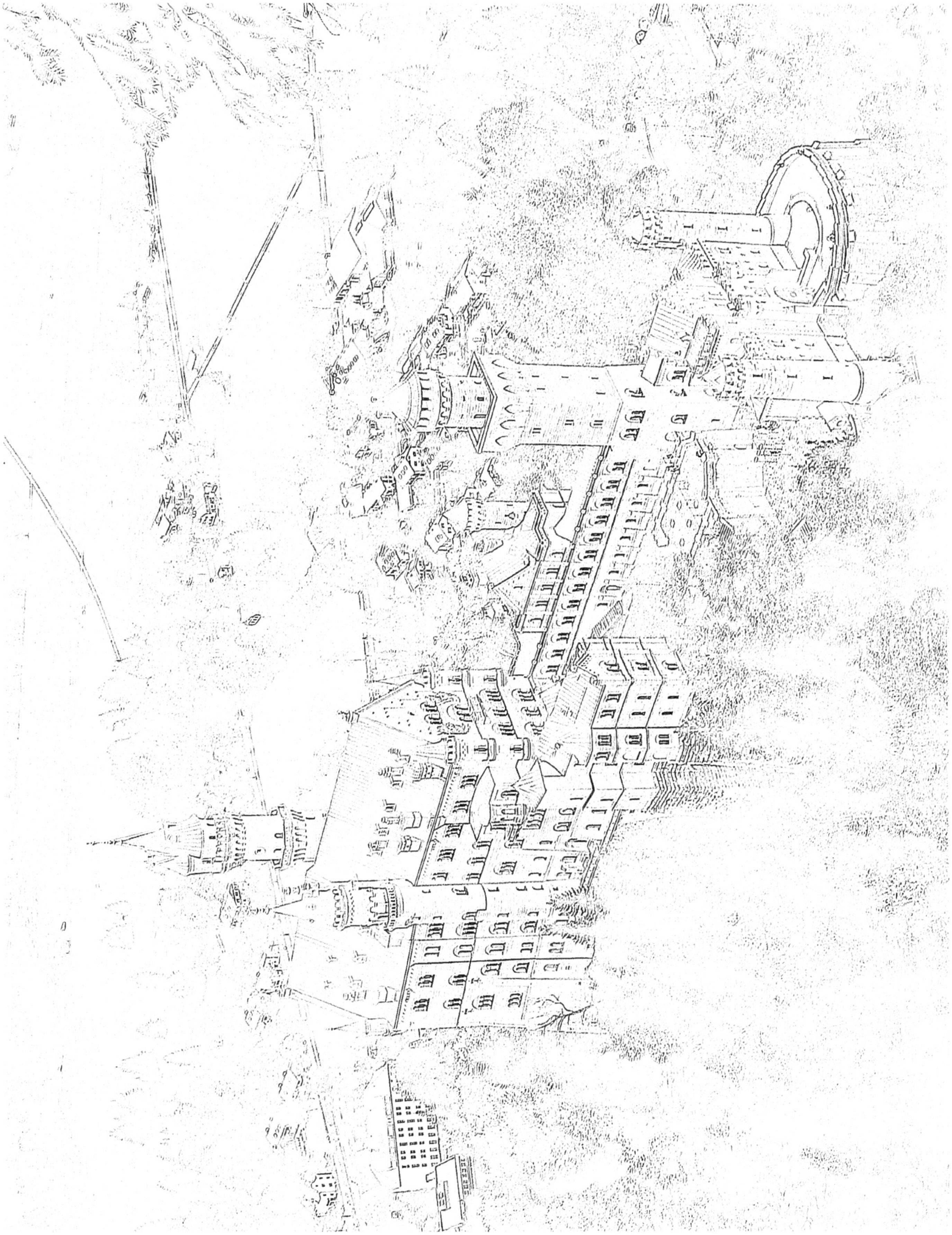

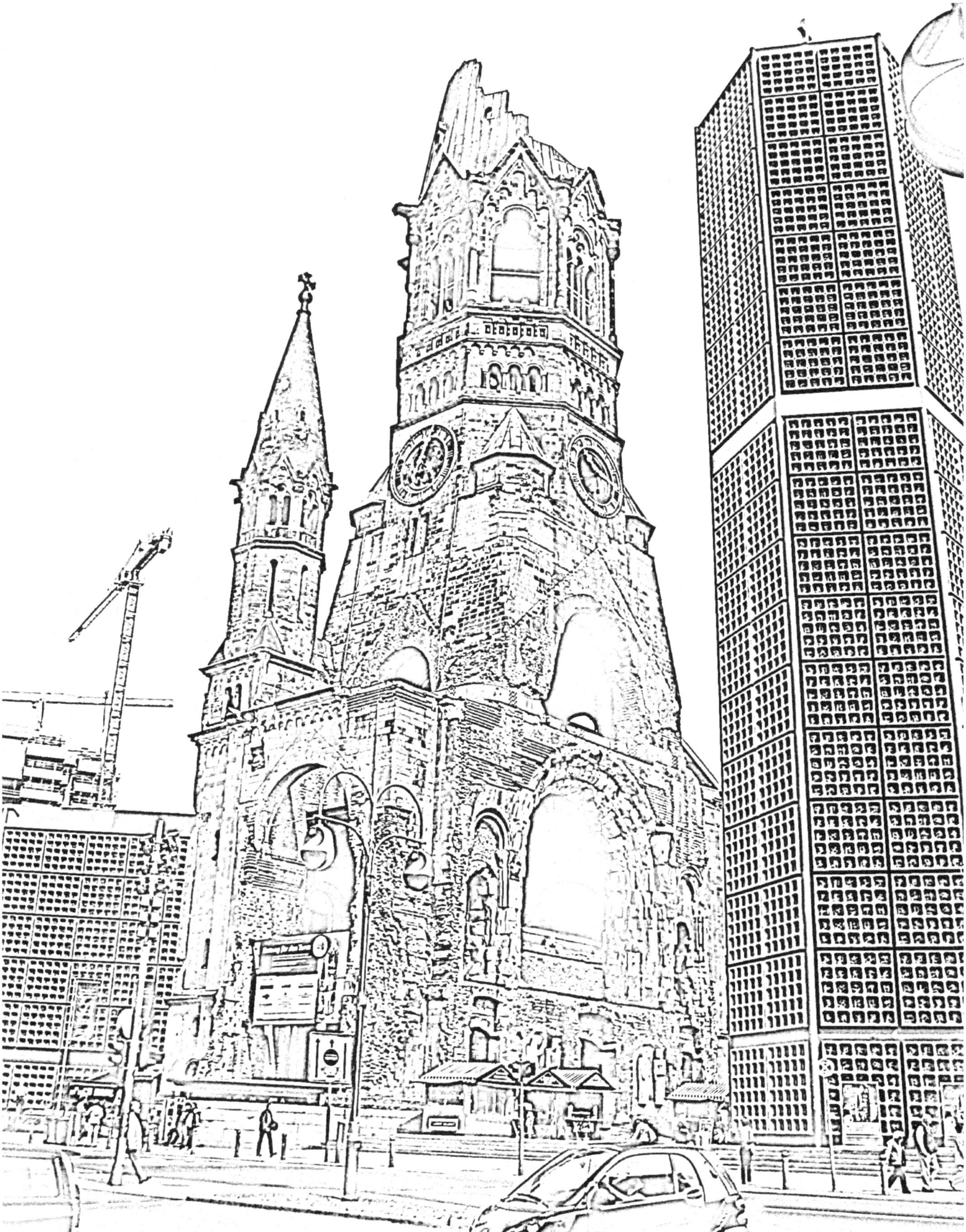

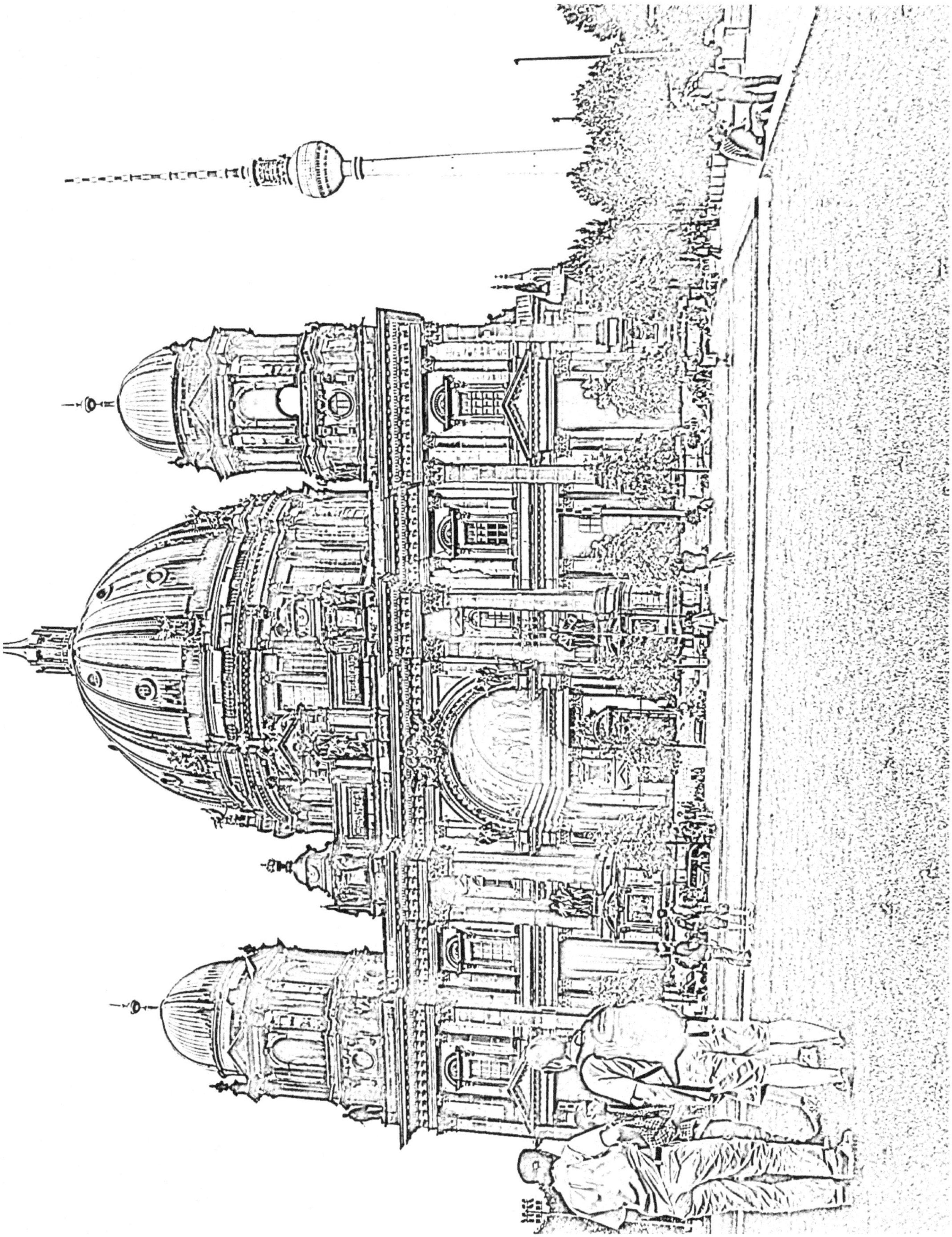

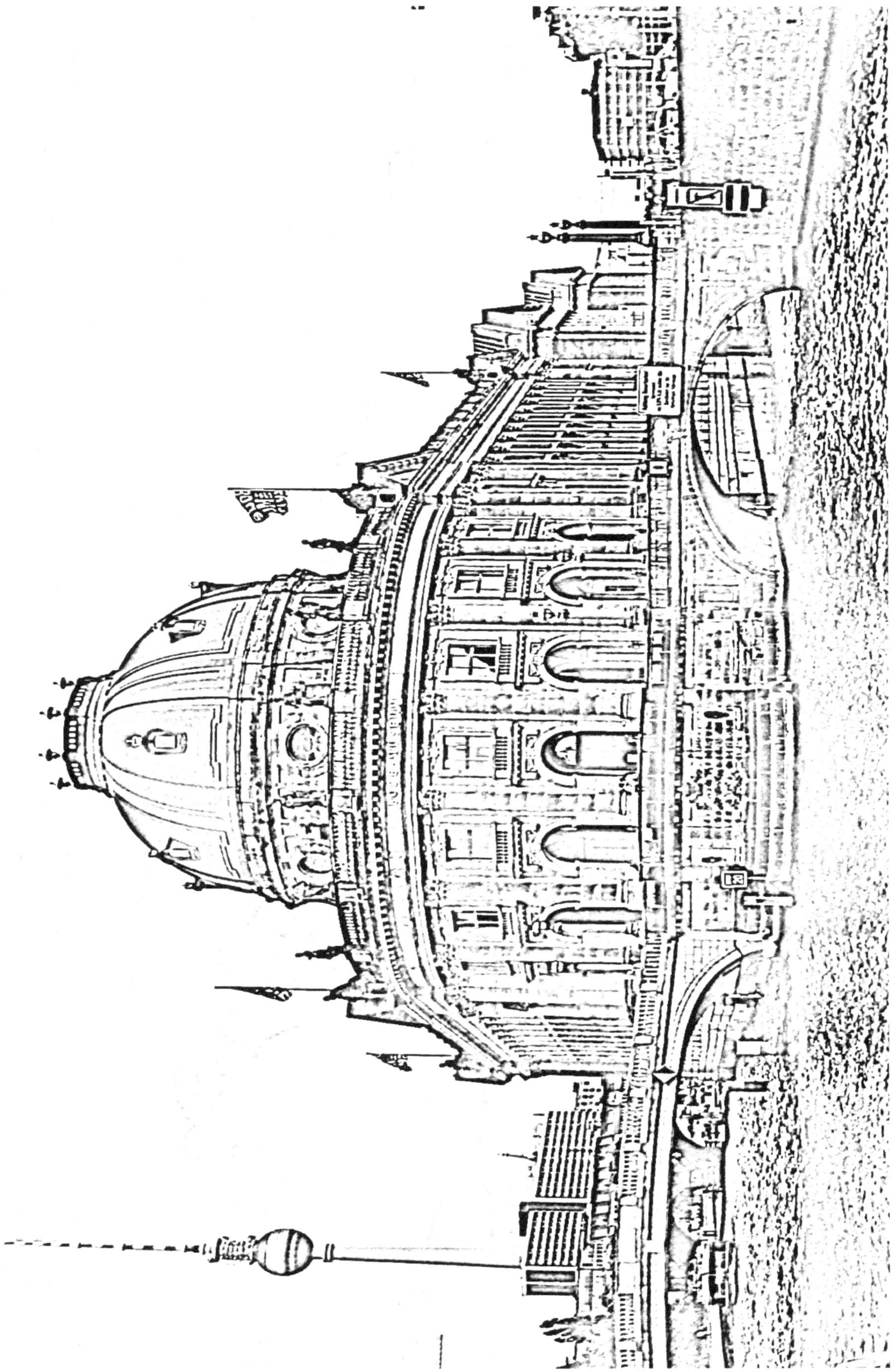

www.ingramcontent.com/pod-product-compliance
Lightning Source LLC
Chambersburg PA
CBHW080608180526
45168CB00007B/2824